A terracotta finial in the shape of a swan on the porch of the entrance lodge at Quarry Park in Shrewsbury.

Ceramic Roofware

Hans van Lemmen

A Shire book

Published in 2003 by Shire Publications Ltd,
Cromwell House, Church Street, Princes Risborough,
Buckinghamshire HP27 9AA, UK.
(Website: www.shirebooks.co.uk)

Copyright © 2003 by Hans van Lemmen.
First published 2003.
Shire Album 420. ISBN 0 7478 0569 5.
Hans van Lemmen is hereby identified as the author of
this work in accordance with Section 77 of the Copyright,
Designs and Patents Act 1988.

British Library Cataloguing in Publication Data:
Van Lemmen, Hans
Ceramic roofware. – (Shire album; 420)
1. Tiles, Roofing – Great Britain – History
2. Brick chimneys – Great Britain – History
3. Decoration and ornament, Architectural –
Great Britain – History
I. Title
738.6'0941
ISBN 0 7478 0569 5

Cover: *A dragon finial on a late-Victorian house on the corner of Headingley Mount and North Lane, Headingley, Leeds. A similar finial on a nearby house is shown on page 14.*

ACKNOWLEDGEMENTS
The author is grateful to Dr Richard Tyler for reading and commenting on the manuscript and to Sheila Adam, Chris Blanchett, Jo Connell, Tracey Crawley, Jacqueline Depelle, Tony Herbert, Kenneth and Helen Major, Lynn Pearson, Angella Streluk, Jon Wilson (Shaws of Darwen), and John Hart (Red Bank Manufacturing Company Limited) for their assistance in various ways. Illustrations are acknowledged as follows: The British Museum, page 7; Tony Herbert, page 9 (bottom); Lynn Pearson, page 32 (bottom right); the Red Bank Manufacturing Company Limited, pages 23 (all) and 24 (all); Jon Wilson, page 34 (bottom). All other photographs are from the author's collection.

Printed in Malta by Gutenberg Press Limited, Gudja Road,
Tarxien PLA 19, Malta.

Contents

A terracotta vase on the Belmont public house, on the corner of West Derby Road and Sheil Road, Liverpool, c.1900.

The sumptuous brick and terracotta roof of the Elephant Tearooms, High Street, Sunderland, designed by the architect Frank Caws in 1873–7. The roof has ridge tiles, chimneys, gables, turrets and terracotta sculptures made by the firm of Doulton, some of which are in the form of elephants and gargoyles.

Introduction

Roofware is a much neglected part of our architectural heritage, but the roof is arguably the most important part of a building. Not only does it provide shelter from the elements and an outlet for smoke, but it can also be decorated. Roofs are not easily accessible, and so few people look consciously at rooftops, yet closer scrutiny can reveal a fascinating range of ceramic roof features and ornamentation.

Roofs are made of many types of material, such as thatch, stone, slate and wood, but roofing materials made from fired clay have proved particularly effective and durable. First, and most important, there are clay roof and ridge tiles, which give buildings protection against rain and snow. Second, for ventilation, there are brick chimneys and clay chimney-pots that allow smoke and fumes to escape from wood, coal and gas fires. Third, there are all kinds of

A ceramic Coade-stone sculpture of a lion on the gatehouse of Preston Hall, Pathhead, Midlothian, Scotland, built in 1794.

Above: *Four chimney-pots on a house in Hyde Park, Leeds. The two outer pots are known as 'bishops' and the brown glazed one as a 'crown louvre' pot. The smaller unglazed pot has unusual vertical louvres.*

Left: *Two brick chimneys in the Tudor style on the roof of the Swimming Baths, Bath Street, Chester, built in 1900–1 by the architectural partnership Douglas & Minshull.*

ceramic roof features, including finials, turrets, vases, sculptures, domes and gables, which not only are aesthetic additions but can also define the status, ownership and function of a building.

The history of ceramic roofware goes back to the Greeks and the Romans, who used terracotta tiles and roof ornament on their buildings for functional and decorative purposes. In medieval times the practice of using ceramic roof tiles was revived for palaces and monastic buildings and became more widespread in the fifteenth century when more houses were built using stone or brick. In the sixteenth century tall brick chimneys became a particular feature of the roofs of many large Tudor and Elizabethan manor houses. Chimney-pots became common in the Georgian, Victorian and later periods when coal was used as fuel.

Until the nineteenth century local potteries and tileries made their products by hand and served their local area. In the nineteenth century the use of machinery made mass production possible and big manufacturers came on to the scene who were able to meet a growing demand in Britain's fast expanding cities and distribute their roofware nationwide via the newly built railways.

A terracotta finial and ridge tiles on the roof of a cottage near the West Port, St Andrews, Fife, Scotland, c.1885.

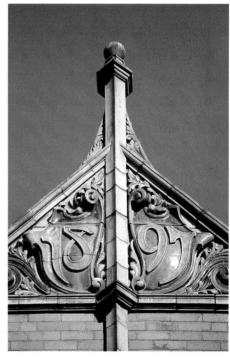

A lion made from glazed faience on the Howard Buildings, Bridge Street, Warrington, Cheshire, c.1905.

The heyday of ceramic roofware in all its forms was the second half of the nineteenth and the early twentieth century. Few buildings great or small were without decorative ridge tiles, chimney-pots or ornamental roofware, which also satisfied the Victorian and Edwardian love of decoration. After the First World War the use of roof ornament lessened because of new architectural tastes and fashions that extolled the virtues of simpler forms with little or no decoration. However, plain chimney-pots and roof tiles continued to be made for the growing number of middle-class suburban homes in the 1920s and 1930s. The use of chimneys and chimney-pots declined sharply after the Second World War when forms of heating other than coal became more common, and many manufacturers of roofware went out of business.

A gable with coloured faience decorations and the date 1897, made by the firm of Burmantoft, on the Grand Arcade, Leeds.

Roof tiles

The Romans introduced ceramic roof tiles into Britain and gave the English language the word 'tile' (from the Latin word *tegula*). After the fall of the Roman Empire the use of ceramic roof tiles ceased and from that time until the twelfth century materials such as thatch or wooden shingles were the most common kinds of roof covering.

From the twelfth century onwards, the use of ceramic roof tiles began to be adopted for prestigious buildings such as abbeys and royal palaces. Their use was also advocated in medieval towns to counter the great fire risk posed by houses with thatched roofs. The medieval roof-tile-maker produced simple flat tiles on a sanded table by rolling out prepared clay and cutting the required shape around a rectangular template or with the aid of a wooden four-sided frame. Holes were made at the top end of the tile through which wooden or iron nails could be pushed to hang the tiles from battens on the roof. Sometimes a small projecting heel was created at the back of the tile near the very top. The tiles would then be hung by hooking the heels over the wooden roof battens. Sometimes both systems were used together – for example, with one nail hole and one projecting heel. More complex roofs needed special tiles such as 'hips' and 'valleys' to cover angles and joints.

Ridge tiles would be moulded into semicircular or triangular shapes and would be used to seal the junctions of sloping roofs. Often the tile-maker would take the opportunity to add decorative features by running an extra strip of clay, which could be cut into ornamental shapes, along the top of the ridge tile. In this way beautiful crests were created, adding striking adornment to

Thirteenth-century roof and ridge tiles in the British Museum, London. The roof tiles on the right and the left are from the site of Clarendon Palace, Wiltshire. The crested ridges in the centre are from the kiln site at Haverholme Priory, Lincolnshire.

Flemish pantiles on an early-seventeenth-century house on The Square in the village of Culross, Fife, Scotland. Culross exported coal and salt to the Low Countries and ships often returned with a ballast of red pantiles.

medieval rooftops. Sometimes the ridge tiles at the end of the roof could be made into very ornate forms known as 'finials', marking the point where the roof met the gable of the building.

From the fifteenth century onwards pantiles made their entry into Britain. At first they were imported from the Low Countries (they are also known as Flemish tiles) but eventually they were also made in Britain. They are 'S' shaped and have a single projecting heel at the top. They were hung by their projecting heel from roof battens without the use of nails but were usually embedded in mortar to make them more secure. Pantiled roofs are still a particular feature of many towns and villages along the east coast of Britain, which used to have direct trading links with Holland and Flanders. The architecturally preserved village of Culross in Fife, Scotland, is an outstanding example.

The former site of the Madeley Wood Company Brick & Tile Works near Ironbridge, Shropshire, where bricks and roof tiles were made during the nineteenth and early twentieth centuries. It is now part of the Blists Hill Open Air Museum.

The roof of the former works office of the Excelsior Tile Works, Chapel Lane, Jackfield, Shropshire, with bands of plain and decorative tiles made by the company.

Coloured glazed tiles arranged in patterns on the roof of a cottage next to the home of the Victorian tile manufacturer Arthur Maw in Ironbridge, Shropshire.

The way roof tiles were produced by hand remained virtually unchanged until the middle of the nineteenth century, when the introduction of machinery reduced manual labour and speeded up output. Steam engines provided power for pug mills and tile-cutting machines, forced drying sheds reduced drying times and kilns increased in size and could be fired with greater accuracy. The Victorian and Edwardian roof-tile industry expanded enormously in areas with good clay deposits. In the Broseley area of Shropshire alone there were forty-five brick and roof-tile manufacturers active during the second half of the nineteenth and the first half of the twentieth century. The Excelsior Tile Works in Jackfield near Broseley, for instance, employed between eighty and ninety men and boys in 1908 and could make about 35,000 roof tiles a day. Although the plain rectangular tile was the most common type produced, it could be made more decorative by cutting the bottom end into different shapes. In this way a roof could be given a more interesting appearance by, for example, alternating bands of plain tiles with decorative ones. Occasionally tiles were glazed and combinations of different-coloured tiles were used to create patterns and designs on the roof.

Red, buff or blue-black ornamental ridge tiles and finials became a common feature on Victorian and Edwardian buildings and even those with slate roofs can have terracotta ridge tiles. Ridge tiles can have many different designs, this being achieved by cutting the top of the crest into various shapes as well as cutting differently shaped openings into it. Because finials have more complex shapes they were manufactured with the aid of plaster moulds. A prototype was first made in clay, from which plaster moulds would be created to produce multiple copies. Firms such as Maw & Company in Jackfield, Shropshire, Haunchwood Brick & Tile Company in Stockingford, Warwickshire, S. & E. Collier in Reading, Berkshire, Barham Brothers in Bridgwater, Somerset, and Prichett & Company in Cowes, Isle of Wight, made a range of decorative ridge tiles and finials.

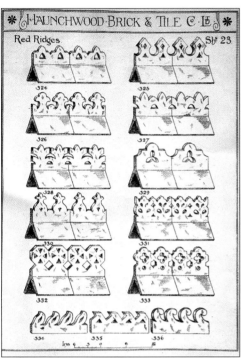

Decorative yellow terracotta ridge tiles on the slate roof of the parish church of St Stephen, Gloucester Road, London SW7, c.1865.

A Haunchwood Brick & Tile Company Limited catalogue page with a selection of decorative ridges, c.1900.

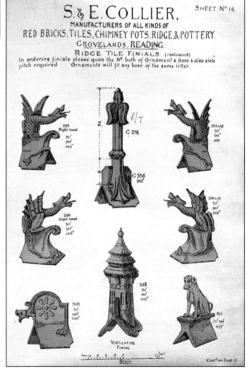

Ornate ridge finials in the catalogue of the Reading firm S. & E. Collier, dated 1899.

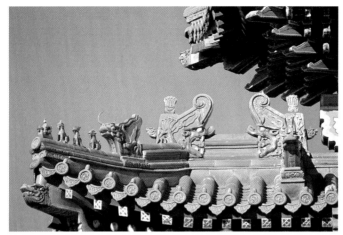

A detail of the elaborate ceramic roof of the Gateway leading into Manchester's Chinatown, constructed c.1975. The glazed tiles and elaborate sculptural ornament provide a glimpse of the long and rich Chinese heritage of ceramic roof decoration.

Right: *The production in the moulding shop of the Red Bank Manufacturing Company at Measham of a clay and plaster replica model of a ridge finial from which plaster working moulds will be made for the production of terracotta finials.*

Left: *A finial on a house in Jackfield, Shropshire. The design of this type of finial is based on a Chinese example.*

Some of the most unusual terracotta finials are in the form of dragons or other animals, and these can still be seen perched on top of Victorian and Edwardian houses throughout Britain. The inspiration for the dragons could have been the fantasy creatures (gargoyles) found on Gothic cathedrals, or perhaps they were influenced by Chinese roofware. The Chinese were renowned for elaborately glazed decorations on the roofs of their palaces, pagodas and city gateways. A glimpse of this can be had in Manchester, where a stunning gate with ornate glazed roofware marks the entrance to Chinatown.

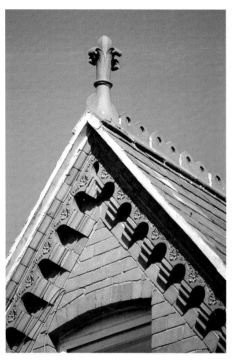

Above left: *The gable of a late-Victorian house in Hoole Road, Chester, with ornate brickwork and a slate roof capped with terracotta ridge tiles and a decorative finial.*

Above right: *A finial in the shape of a bird on the roof of a late-Victorian house in Chalfont Road, Oxford.*

A dragon finial on the roof of a late-Victorian house in Chalfont Road, Oxford.

13

A dragon finial on a late-Victorian house on the corner of Headingley Mount and North Lane, Headingley, Leeds. A similar finial on a neighbouring house is illustrated on the front cover.

Although the fashion for highly decorative ridges and finials declined after the First World War, simple ones continued to be made. They were used on inter-war semi-detached houses, particularly those built in the neo-Tudor style, and have made a reappearance in some contemporary housing estates, in which semi-detached homes are built mimicking the style of the 1920s and 1930s.

Brick chimneys

The history of the chimney goes back to the Romans, who used flues made from hollow bricks to let smoke escape from the fires that heated their bath-houses via small terracotta chimneys on the roof. The Saxons had a hearth on an earth floor in the middle of their huts in which they burned wood or peat, and the smoke would be allowed to escape either of its own accord or by being drawn away through a smoke hole in the thatched roof. When the Normans came to Britain in 1066 things changed. They began to build defensive keeps consisting of thick stone walls with wooden floors. For safety reasons the living quarters would be on the first floor and, since lighting fires on a wooden floor was not practical, the Normans would hollow out a section in the wall to make a hearth. The smoke would be drawn off via a flue and escape through openings higher up in the wall.

When from the twelfth century onwards castles, palaces and abbeys were built with stone, the construction of wall fireplaces became more prevalent. The flues in the walls became longer and some even reached roof level, at which point they were surmounted by a round stone shaft. It is in this way that the first roof chimneys were created. Here we have arrived at the prototype of all standard chimney design: a hearth for the fire, a flue to take smoke up through the wall, and an external structure on top of the roof to let smoke escape well clear of the roof.

The open hearth in the middle of the room for the burning of wood, turf or charcoal was not altogether abandoned. Throughout the Middle Ages its use continued in some halls and manor houses, and ventilation was improved by means of a smoke louvre built on the roof. These were vertical structures usually made from wood with angled slats in their sides that would create an updraught and so facilitate the escape of smoke. The use of smoke louvres as a part of chimney-pot design will be discussed later. In medieval towns chimneys could be made of wattle and daub or of plaster of Paris mixed with mortar, which were less of a fire risk. In the fifteenth century it became more common to use fireproof bricks for the construction of chimneys and this became the preferred material for the great brick chimneys of the Tudor and Elizabethan age and later periods.

In the sixteenth century the pre-eminent building with brick chimneys was Hampton Court near London. Construction began around 1515 under Thomas Wolsey, the Lord Chancellor. The chimneys on the roof of Hampton Court consist of three components, the base, the shaft and the cap, and some are up to 14 feet (4.3 metres) high. Various kinds of moulded bricks were used in their

Ornate brick chimneys on the roof of Hampton Court, near London. They are for the most part exact replacements of the early-sixteenth-century originals.

construction and some of the shafts have chevron, diamond or honeycomb patterns, while others look like pieces of twisted barley sugar. The caps are rounded, polygonal, star-shaped or battlemented. The majority of chimneys at Hampton Court have been restored with new bricks but they are exact replacements and are still one of the great architectural features of the building.

Hampton Court set a trend for brick chimneys followed by many members of the nobility, for whom having them on their manor houses became something of a status symbol. Most rooms in large houses at that time would have a fireplace connected to a brick chimney on the roof. The more chimneys on the roof, the more rooms in the house. A number of Tudor manor houses with chimneys have survived, for example the magnificent East Barsham Hall in Norfolk, built between 1525 and 1535. This house has numerous imposing decorative brick chimneys, of which many are original rather than restored. There is one stack with a cluster of ten chimney shafts (they have lost their caps), creating an impressive crowning feature to the roof. Norfolk also offers a range of less

The sixteenth-century brick façade of Denver Hall, Denver, Norfolk, with its crow-step gable, turrets and chimneys.

Sixteenth-century brick chimneys and turrets on the roof of the Tudor manor house at Great Snoring, Norfolk. All the chimneys except one have lost their caps.

Below: *Sixteenth-century chimneys on the roof of Plaish Hall, Longville, Shropshire. The shape of their caps is known as a 'midland star'.*

exalted examples of Tudor architecture, which are still worth seeking out, such as Denver Hall and the Tudor manor house at Great Snoring.

Brick chimneys with an unusual tale attached to them can be found on the roof of Plaish Hall, near Longville in Shropshire, which was built *c.*1540 by Sir William Leighton, a judge at Shrewsbury assize. When a man appeared before him accused of stealing sheep he condemned him to hang. On hearing that the man was a skilled bricklayer Leighton took him back to his manor, which was under construction, and set him to building brick chimneys. Nevertheless, when the job was done the man was taken back to Shrewsbury and executed. Until this day the chimneys at Plaish Hall are known as the 'hanging chimneys'.

17

An Elizabethan brick chimney with star-shaped caps on the roof of Benthall Hall, Benthall, Shropshire. By the end of the sixteenth century chimneys had become plainer and were little more than tall brick stacks.

The design of brick chimneys became simpler over time and already by the end of the sixteenth century the shafts of chimneys were often nothing more than plain polygonal brick stacks with moulded caps. A good example of this trend can be seen at Benthall Hall, Shropshire, which is a stone-built house with three tall brick chimneys with star-shaped caps, dating from the 1580s. By 1600 the heyday of the large brick chimney-stack was over when the classical style became the norm for grand houses, built in stone rather than brick.

At the end of the eighteenth and the beginning of the nineteenth century, when the Gothic style came back into fashion, Tudor-type chimneys made a comeback – but they were not necessarily made of brick. The firm of Mrs Eleanor Coade in London produced terracotta chimneys in the Tudor style from a white-grey ceramic material that looked like stone. The chimneys were

Below left: Coade-stone chimneys in the Tudor style on the roof of Dalmeny House, Dalmeny, Midlothian, Scotland, built in 1814–17.

Coade-stone chimneys on Henry VII Lodge, Woburn Sands, Buckinghamshire, 1810–11. They are based on the Tudor chimneys at East Barsham Hall in Norfolk.

18

produced in sections and assembled on the roof. Good examples can still be seen on the roof of Dalmeny House, near Edinburgh, built in 1814–17, and on Henry VII Lodge, Woburn Sands, Buckinghamshire, erected in 1810–11.

The brick chimney as a dominant external feature of the roof also became a hallmark of some Gothic Revival architects, such as George Gilbert Scott, and Arts and Crafts architects, such as Richard Norman Shaw. Scott's interest in massive brick chimneys can be seen on the roof of St Pancras station, London, constructed

Above: *A joint stack of four brick chimneys enriched with terracotta 'paterae' and capped with simple yellow pots on a Victorian house in Fitzwilliam Avenue, Belfast.*

Right: *One of the massive brick chimney-stacks at Lowther Lodge, South Kensington, London, designed by Richard Norman Shaw in 1874.*

19

Above left: *An ornate terracotta chimney-stack with baroque decorations on a block of shops and houses in South Audley Street, Mayfair, London, designed by the architect A. J. Bolton in 1893.*

Above right: *A chimney-stack with an Italianate design, made from brown glazed faience blocks, at 39 Brompton Road, London, c.1900. It is abutted by a brick stack of an earlier date with simple 'roll-top' chimney-pots.*

in 1866–71. Shaw had a penchant for placing brick chimneys against the outer walls, along which they rise up from ground level and project at great height above the roof, creating imposing vertical features. His Lowther Lodge, built in South Kensington, London, in 1874, is a case in point. Scott and Shaw influenced other architects, as can be seen in the model village of Port Sunlight, Wirral, founded in 1888, where massive brick chimneys are striking features of many houses.

An assortment of brick chimneys in the Tudor and Elizabethan styles capped with chimney-pots on houses in Port Sunlight, Wirral, c.1895.

Chimney-pots

As we have seen, the history of the chimney-pot goes back to Roman times and there is also archaeological evidence that small clay chimney-pots were used on medieval houses. These were made of unglazed buff or reddish-brown clay and were between 12 and 18 inches (30 and 45 cm) high, slightly tapering towards the top. Examples have been found at Chichester and Lewes in Sussex. However, it was not until Georgian times that the clay chimney-pot came into its own, when it started to be used to top chimney-stacks on buildings in which coal was burned for heating and cooking.

The switch from burning wood to burning coal had implications for the design of fireplaces, the flues and the chimneys on the roof. Wood can simply be burned in an open hearth supported by firedogs, but when coal is burned it has to be raised from the hearth floor to let sufficient air circulate and to let burnt ashes fall away at the bottom of the fire. Special metal firegrates were designed for this purpose and the flues were made narrower above the grate to create a stronger updraught to expel the noxious and dangerous fumes of coal fires. The designing of chimney places, which would allow heat in the room but draw off the smoke more efficiently, became a serious business. A treatise on the subject written by Count Rumford was published in 1797 and led to great improvements. Chimney-stacks on the roof and the introduction of chimney-pots also played an important part in creating more effective means of smoke outlet. Most Georgian and Victorian buildings would have a fireplace in every room and the chimneys on the roof became joined multiple stacks made of stone or brick, providing outlets for flues. In densely built-up areas air currents can eddy around buildings and create down-draughts. Chimney-pots were placed on the chimney-stacks to create more updraught.

Georgian chimney-pots were 'thrown' by hand on a potter's wheel. They were usually about 2 feet (60 cm) high or roughly as long as the arm of the potter, who needed to reach inside during the pot's production. Taller pots could be made if needed by joining together separately thrown pieces. Chimney-pots were made from buff or red firing clay and were left unglazed. A simple roll top was a common finishing feature, but potters added decoration by stamping designs in the clay or painting rings around the pot using white slip. Georgian pots can be recognised by their somewhat uneven look and ring marks left by the potter.

A handmade Georgian chimney-pot on a brick stack of an outbuilding in School Alley, Wells-next-the-Sea, Norfolk. The potter has added some simple impressed decorations near the top of the pot.

Four handmade Georgian chimney-pots with simple crown decorations have survived on a stone stack at Aynam Lodge, Aynam Road, Kendal, Cumbria, built by the architect Francis Webster in 1824. The four red replacement pots are in keeping with the originals.

Victorian pots were made from white, buff or red firing clay. To improve the colour of the red pots they were sometimes dipped into red slip. Chimney-pots were made in different ways and three main production processes can be identified. First, there is the use of the extrusion machine employed for the production of cylindrical pipes, which could easily be fashioned into chimney-pots. Second, pots with more complex shapes were press-moulded. In this process clay is pressed into a plaster mould to a thickness of about 1 inch (2.5 cm) and the clay is left to dry. When the clay is leather-hard, the mould is removed and the pot is finished by hand. The bases and tops of more ornate pots were made separately from the main shaft and then joined together. Third, pots could be slip-cast, which involved the pouring of liquid clay (slip) into plaster moulds. After a period of drying the moulds were removed and the pots finished by

A smoking chimney with a buff single-beaded 'can' on a cottage dating from 1832 at The Crescent, Dura Den, Fife, Scotland.

An extrusion machine in operation, used for the manufacture of chimney shafts and flue linings at the Red Bank Manufacturing Company Limited.

Above: *A workman engaged in press-moulding square chimney-pots in plaster moulds at Red Bank.*

A workman fitting a 'hood' on top of a square chimney-pot with 'pockets' at Red Bank.

23

The slip-cast bottom section of a 'bishop' chimney-pot in the process of being removed from the mould at the Red Bank Manufacturing Company Limited.

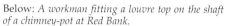

Below: *A workman fitting a louvre top on the shaft of a chimney-pot at Red Bank.*

Left: *Handwork is still an essential part of chimney-pot manufacture, for example with the cutting of openings into a louvre top, at Red Bank.*

hand. Most chimney-pots were left unglazed but in some areas such as Yorkshire they could be given a covering of brown salt glaze, making them more weather-resistant.

Many manufacturers, large and small, produced chimney-pots. Firms including Julius Whitehead & Sons in Bradford, A. Harris &

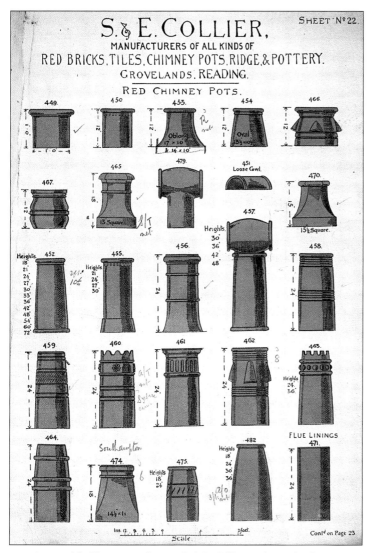

A page with chimney-pots from an S. & E. Collier catalogue, dated 1899.

Son in Wrecclesham, Surrey, Gunton Brothers in Costessey near Norwich, J. M. Blashfield in Stamford, Lincolnshire, S. & E. Collier in Reading and Haunchwood Brick & Tile Company in Stockingford, Warwickshire, would distribute their wares mainly in the areas in which they were situated. Large concerns such as Doulton in London, J. C. Edwards in Ruabon, Wrexham, Gibbs & Canning in Tamworth, Staffordshire, and the Leeds Fireclay Company in Yorkshire supplied customers both in their own region and

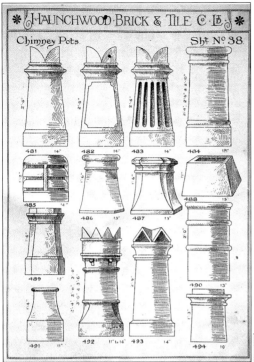

A page with chimney-pots from a Haunchwood Brick & Tile Company Limited catalogue, c.1900. Number 485 is a louvre top, while number 492 is a 'bishop' pot.

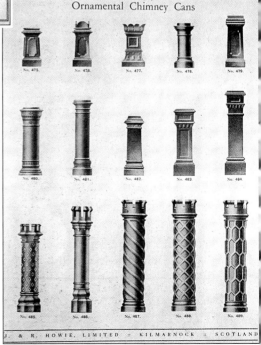

A page with 'Ornamental Chimney Cans' from a catalogue of the Scottish firm J. & R. Howie Limited, c.1925. Even at this late date some very ornate pots were still being made. The five pots at the bottom of the page are reminiscent of Tudor chimneys.

elsewhere throughout the nation using Britain's extensive railway system. Chimney-pots were also made in Scotland (where they are called 'chimney cans') by firms such as J. & R. Howie, Hurlford, Kilmarnock, and the Glenboig Union Fireclay Company Limited, Glenboig, North Lanarkshire. The catalogues of all these firms provide useful insight into the range of chimney-pots produced and the names given to specific types of pot.

Although chimney-pots can have intriguing shapes their design is in the first instance driven by practical concerns. The main function of a chimney-pot is to increase updraught in the flue, and this can be made more effective by adding extra openings cut into the bottom, middle or top of the pot to create upward air currents. These openings are known as 'horns', 'pockets' or 'louvres' depending on their shape and position. Pots with such extra additions are also referred to as 'smoke cures'. A semicircular clay 'hood' or 'saddle' can be placed on the chimney-pot to prevent rain and snow going down the flue and to prevent down-draught. If chimney-stacks were well below the lee of a neighbouring roof or next to a much higher

Below left: Two unusual chimney-pots in High Gate, Kendal, Cumbria. The unglazed pot has 'handles' at the top and the glazed pot on the right has 'horns' at the bottom and a single louvre opening near the top below the crown. All these devices are aids for increasing updraught.

Below right: A stack with two chimney-pots on an outbuilding at St Mary's Hill, Stamford, Lincolnshire. The local firm Blashfield probably made the unglazed square pot, but the brown salt-glazed pot is a later product, known as a 'champion' or 'smoke cure', with vents at the bottom.

Three 'beehive' chimney-pots on a late-Victorian house in Canal Street, as seen from the city walls of Chester. The two larger ones have 'pockets' for extra updraught.

stack, very long pots of up to 6 or 7 feet (about 2 metres) high, known as 'tall boys', were placed on the lower stack to catch the wind.

In addition to the practical matters of design, chimney-pots can also be highly decorative accoutrements to a building. If Georgian pots are very simple, early-Victorian pots copy the intricate design of Tudor chimneys and by the 1860s a multitude of different designs had been developed to ornament the roofs of buildings.

Above: *Two 'tall boys' on a building in Broad Street, Reading, Berkshire, have been used to bridge the gap between a low and a high stack, c.1900. The chimney-pots were probably made by the local firm S. & E. Collier.*

Right: *The roof of a mid-nineteenth-century cottage in Headingley, Leeds, with buff Tudor-style terracotta chimney-pots.*

A series of buff square chimney-pots with classical ornamentation on a house on the corner of Westfield Avenue and the West Port, Cupar, Fife, Scotland, c.1870.

The distinctive shapes of chimney-pots also led to them being given certain names. Pots with crowns are known as 'bishops'; tall, round pots with pockets and castellated tops are called 'knights' because they look like giant chess pieces. Pots with something like an inverted flowerpot on top are labelled 'buckets', while short, simple, round pots tapering towards the top are known as 'beehives'. Chimney-pots with special top sections with three or more angled clay slats are named 'louvres' because they are reminiscent of the medieval wooden louvres

Above: *The rooftops of late-nineteenth-century houses in Wycliffe Road, Rodley, West Yorkshire, dominated by stone stacks with salt-glazed chimney-pots, the majority of which are either 'knights' or 'bishops'.*

Left: *A brick stack with late-nineteenth-century salt-glazed chimney-pots in Hyde Park, Leeds. The two pots on the left are called 'bishops' and the one on the right is known as a 'fluted double roll-top'.*

29

covering smoke holes. The sheer variety of chimney-pots is enormous and runs into hundreds of different types if combinations of shape and variations of height are taken into consideration.

Chimney-pots set high on brick or stone stacks are striking images and have even inspired poets to put pen to paper. The magazine *Claycraft* published a poem by Frank S. Russell in the October issue of 1943 called 'Ode to a Chimney Pot', of which the last five stanzas are extracted below.

Without thee, food might go uncooked,
Our room unventilated,
Perchance their faces black with smoke,
Our babes be suffocated!

So, Hail to England's Chimney Pots,
That baffle the Undertaker,
But most of all, in gratitude
God bless the Chimney Pot maker!

Who to a lump of slimy clay
Brings, Science, Faith and Skill,
Capital, Courage, Patience,
And bends them to his will.

Then proved by fire, both round and smooth,
Thy skin rewards his pains,
The Builder sets thee proud on high,
Where washed by endless rains.

A hundred years before thee,
Though thine heart be black and hot,
Thy trials never ending – thou'llt
Stand Firm and fast my Pot!

A salt-glazed 'knight' chimney-pot now serving as a giant flower-holder in a garden in Headingley, Leeds.

Replicas of Victorian chimney-pots such as this magnificent crown louvre pot with 'horns' are still made by the Red Bank Manufacturing Company in Measham.

Unfortunately, chimney-pots were not to stand firm for much longer. In 1952 London suffered from terrible smog and at least four thousand people died of respiratory illness. The government passed new legislation and the result was the Clean Air Act of 1956, which set up smokeless zones in all major cities. Coal as a main form of household fuel in urban areas became a thing of the past and was replaced by electric or gas-fired central heating. Chimney places were bricked up or taken out and flues and pots fell into disuse. The modernisation of inner cities in the 1960s and 1970s resulted in the clearance of many areas with Victorian houses and the subsequent destruction of chimneys and their pots. However, sometimes the artistic merits of chimney-pots were recognised and they were saved and sold on as garden ornaments when houses were demolished. Stacks and chimney-pots are making a comeback in new housing estates as part of the trend for 'live' imitation coal fires run on gas. There is again a growing market for chimney-pots, which is well catered for by firms such as the Red Bank Manufacturing Company of Measham, Swadlincote, Derbyshire, who are also involved in the restoration of historic buildings and the making of replicas of old chimney-pots.

A terracotta Coade-stone sculpture of a sphinx on Dunbar Castle, Dunbar, East Lothian, 1790.

Decorative features

A terracotta Coade-stone sculpture of Britannia by the modeller John C. F. Rossi on Liverpool Town Hall, c.1795.

Ceramic roof decorations can appear in many guises, such as sculptures, ornamental domes, decorative pediments and ornate gables. In Britain ceramic roof sculpture of any significance first appeared during the second half of the eighteenth century when the Coade factory was set up in London in 1769. Coade made architectural ornaments of white-grey terracotta known as 'Coade stone', which closely resembled limestone in texture and colour. Architects such as James Wyatt, Robert Adam and Robert Mitchell used Coade-stone decorations and sculptures for their neo-classical buildings to act as symbols of prestige and ownership. Robert Adam built Dunbar Castle, East Lothian, Scotland, for the eighth Earl of Lauderdale in 1790 and placed a sphinx (the crest of the Earl) of

A terracotta Coade-stone lion dated 1837 from the roof of the former Lion Brewery in London. It now stands on Westminster Bridge, London.

32

Coade stone on the top of the façade. Also in Scotland, Robert Mitchell used Coade-stone lions on the roof of the impressive entrance gates to Preston Hall near Edinburgh in 1794. When Wyatt rebuilt the Liverpool town hall in 1795 he specially ordered for the top of the dome a large Coade-stone sculpture of Britannia, which is still in place today. A Coade-stone lion, dated 1837, that once stood on the roof of the Lion Brewery, Westminster, in London, was saved when the brewery was demolished in the 1950s and can now be found guarding the entrance to Westminster Bridge. Terracotta lions of a different kind can be found on the roof of the former Phipps Brewery in Stamford, Lincolnshire, where they still support the brewery's trade-mark made by the local terracotta manufacturer J. M. Blashfield in 1871.

Terracotta manufacturers also produced ceramic roof sculptures. The highly ornate Law Courts in Birmingham designed by Aston Webb and Ingress Bell were completed in 1891. The whole edifice is constructed from pink-red terracotta made by J. C. Edwards. Its façade is festooned with terracotta sculptures and ornament but the most striking one, perched high on the roof, is a figure symbolising Justice designed by the sculptor W. S. Frith. The façades of music-halls, theatres and early cinemas were sometimes decorated with faience sculptures representing muses. Examples include Frank Matcham's Hackney Empire, Mare Street, London, built in 1901 with a figure of the Greek muse Euterpe standing on top of the façade. It was made by the Hathern Station Brick and Terracotta Company. The

The terracotta statue of Justice on the Law Courts, Corporation Street, Birmingham, modelled by the sculptor W. S. Frith and made by J. C. Edwards, 1891.

Above left: A faience statue representing the Greek muse Euterpe, probably made by the Leeds firm Burmantoft, on the Tower Cinema in Hull, 1914.

Above right: An heraldic griffin made of Burmantoft terracotta on the roof of the County Arcade, Leeds, 1900.

Edwardian Tower Cinema in Hull, dating from 1914, also has a statue of the muse Euterpe but here she is sitting on the edge of the façade dressed in flowing robes reminiscent of the Art Nouveau style. There are also many less exalted examples of ceramic roof sculpture and ornament. Throughout the British Isles there are late-

A view of the roof of the Hackney Empire, Mare Street, London, with its two ornamental faience domes and the statue of the Greek muse Euterpe, made by the Hathern Station Brick and Terracotta Company in 1901 but completely restored by Shaws of Darwen in 1988.

34

nineteenth-century and early-twentieth-century shops, offices and public houses embellished with ceramic lions, griffins, urns and vases, adding a touch of opulence to the roof.

A small number of buildings have ornamental domes or cupolas made from unglazed terracotta or glazed faience. They are usually found on shopping arcades, department stores, theatres, music-halls and circuses dating from around 1900 and complement the sumptuous baroque styles employed for these buildings. In Leeds, for example, there are the County Arcades designed by Frank Matcham with glazed ornamental domes and cupolas made by the local firm Burmantoft in 1900. In London there is the sumptuous terracotta dome crowning Harrod's Department Store in Knightsbridge designed by the architectural partnership Stevens & Hunt and built in 1901–5, while in Great Yarmouth can be found the exuberant Hippodrome, designed

Above: *An ornate terracotta and faience dome with baroque decoration on the County Arcade, Leeds, made by Burmantoft in 1900.*

One of the terracotta domes with Art Nouveau detailing on the roof of the Hippodrome in Great Yarmouth, Norfolk; made by Doulton, 1903.

by Ralph Scott Cockrill and opened in 1903 for circus entertainment. Doulton probably made the two terracotta domes with their Art Nouveau decorations.

Decorative gables with ceramic embellishments are a feature of many late-Victorian and Edwardian buildings. They can carry the name of the building, the date of construction, images that relate to its function or ownership, or just decorative features to enrich the roof. Dormer windows often have a small gable above the window area that can be filled with ornamental tiles or terracotta/faience

Above left: The imposing terracotta dome of Harrod's Department Store, Knightsbridge, London, 1901–5.

Above right: A large corner turret made of Burmantoft faience on the roof of Lancaster House, Whitworth Street, Manchester, 1906.

A terracotta gable with a pterodactyl on the Natural History Museum in London; made by Gibbs & Canning, 1873–81.

Above: *A dormer with a gable, decorated with encaustic tiles and the date 1880, in Regent Road, Great Yarmouth, Norfolk.*

Left: *An ornamental terracotta dormer with the statue of an elephant on the Elephant Tearooms in the High Street, Sunderland; made by Doulton 1873–7.*

decorations. Important examples include the Natural History Museum (1873–81) in London, designed by Alfred Waterhouse, which has interesting terracotta gables featuring extinct animals and made by the firm Gibbs & Canning. The Elephant Tearooms (1873–7) in Sunderland, designed by Frank Caws, has small dormers projecting from between the gables of the façade and containing charming terracotta sculptures of elephants made by Doulton. Colourful gable ends with Art Nouveau decorations made from coloured Carraraware manufactured by Doulton can be found on the Royal Arcades (1899) in Norwich, designed by G. J. Skipper, and on top of the Turkey Café (1901) in Leicester, designed by A. Wakerley.

Roof sculptures, domes, pediments and gable ends are less common than roof tiles, brick

One of the dormers with elaborate terracotta decorations in the late-Gothic style on a group of houses in Cross Street, Port Sunlight, Wirral, by the architectural partnership Grayson & Ould, 1896.

chimneys and chimney-pots, but they are eye-catching. The history of ceramic roofware is full of objects that have added interest and often colour to the roofs of buildings throughout the British Isles. Only a representative sample has been covered in this introductory account, which maps out the field, but anyone who is interested in the roofscapes that give British towns and cities their unique appearance can and will discover his or her own local favourites.

A gable with Art Nouveau decorations executed in coloured Carraraware by Doulton on the Royal Arcade, Norwich, 1899.

Glossary

Beehive: a squat chimney-pot with a slightly rounded top reminiscent of a straw beehive.

Bishop: a round chimney-pot with a square base and the top section cut into triangles reminiscent of a bishop's mitre.

Bucket: a round chimney-pot with a top that looks like an inverted bucket.

Cap: the decorative top section of a Tudor or Elizabethan brick chimney.

Carraraware: weather-resistant white or coloured faience material made by Doulton for the exterior of buildings.

Chimney: a vertical channel conducting smoke or gases up and away from a fire through a flue and emitting it clear of the building via a section of the chimney that projects above the roof.

Chimney-pot: a clay pipe at the top of a chimney narrowing the aperture and increasing updraught.

Chimney-stack: a single chimney or a number of chimneys grouped into one brick or stone structure usually containing several flues.

Coade stone: a type of white-grey terracotta made by the Coade stone factory in London between 1769 and 1838 and used for architectural ornament and chimneys.

Cupola: a small dome adorning a roof.

Dome: a curved roof with a round or polygonal base.

Dormer: a projecting upright window in a sloping roof.

Faience: terracotta covered with semi-translucent or opaque glazes.

Finial: an ornament finishing off the apex of a roof or the gable.

Firedog: a metal support for burning wood in a fireplace.

Fireplace: a place for a domestic fire at the base of the chimney.

Gable: the triangular upper part of an exterior wall between the slopes of the roof.

Grate: the recess of a fireplace in the chimney *or* a metal frame set into the recess containing coal.

Hearth: the floor of a fireplace *or* the fireproof area in front of a fireplace.

Heel: a protruding flange or lip at the top of a roof tile so that it can be hung from roof battens.

Hood: a semicircular piece of fired clay placed across the top of a chimney-pot to keep out the rain and prevent downdraught. It is sometimes also called a 'saddle'.

Horns: round projections protruding from the bottom of a chimney-pot and slanted downwards to create extra updraught.

Knight: a tall round chimney-pot with a castellated top and pockets protruding from the sides, making it look like a giant chess piece.

Louvre: a series of inclined horizontal slats set in a vertical frame allowing ventilation without letting in rain. In medieval times they were sometimes set over holes in the roof to draw off smoke from a central hearth. Horizontal clay slats became a common feature in the tops of round chimney-pots to help increase updraught.

Midland star: a star-shaped cap found on Tudor and Elizabethan brick chimneys that is particularly common in the Midlands.

Pantile: a large roof tile shaped like an S in cross-section.

Pocket: a small protrusion at the side of a chimney-pot creating a small opening to help increase updraught.

Ridge tiles: triangular or semicircular tiles that are used to cover the line of junction of two parts of the roof sloping upwards to each other.

Roof tiles: flat or curved clay tiles overlapping or interlocking with other tiles hung from or nailed to wooden battens on the roof. They can have various shapes and are usually unglazed.

Slip: liquid clay used in the production of chimney-pots made in plaster moulds in a process known as 'slip casting'.

Tall boy: a very tall chimney-pot.

Terracotta: unglazed red or buff fired clay.

Turret: a small tower decorating a building.

Further reading

Barnard, Julian. *The Decorative Tradition*. The Architectural Press, 1973.

Bennett, Frank, and Pinion, Alfred. *Roof Slating and Tiling*. The Caxton Publishing Company Limited, 1935 (reprinted 1960).

Chatham, John H. *Going to Pot? The Great British Chimney*. Baron Birch, 1995.

Fletcher, Valentine. *Chimney Pots and Stacks: An Introduction to Their History, Variety and Identification*. Centaur Press Limited, 1968.

Hammond, Martin. 'Hand-made manufacture of terracotta chimney pots', *Glazed Expressions*, 22 (Spring 1991).

Kelly, Alison. *Mrs Coade's Stone*. The Self Publishing Association Limited, 1990.

Leitch, Kerry, and Smith, Martin. *Chimney Trail*. Stamford Museum Town Trail, 1986.

Mugridge, A. J. *The Broseley Heavy Clay Industry with Particular Reference to Brickyards and Roof Tile Manufactories*. Privately published by A. J. Mugridge, Telford, 2001.

Wight, Jane A. *Brick Building in England from the Middle Ages to 1550*. John Baker, 1972.

Places to visit

The British Museum, Great Russell Street, London WC1B 3DG. Telephone: 020 7323 8000 or 020 7323 8299. Website: www.thebritishmuseum.ac.uk.

Jackfield Tile Museum, Ironbridge Gorge, Telford, Shropshire TF8 7DQ. Telephone: 01952 432166. Website: www.ironbridge.org.uk (Part of Ironbridge Gorge Museum.)

Park Farm Museum, Milton Abbas, Dorset DT11 0AX. Telephone: 01258 880828. Website: www.parkfarmcottages.co.uk

Stamford Museum, Broad Street, Stamford PE9 1PJ. Telephone: 01780 766317. Website: www.lincolnshire.gov.uk

---

Tiles and Architectural Ceramics Society. Secretary: Kath Adams, Oakhurst, Cocknage Road, Rough Close, Stoke-on-Trent, Staffordshire ST3 7NN. Website: www.tilesoc.org.uk

The top section of the Turkey Café, Granby Street, Leicester (1900–1), executed in coloured Carraraware by Doulton.